Throwaway Child

The Life of John A. Garrison

As told to

JOYCE C. RAGLAND

Paperback-Press
an imprint of A & S Publishing
A & S Holmes, Inc.

ISBN: 069222367-3
ISBN-13: 978-0-692-22367-3

DEDICATION

This book is dedicated to all children whose parents did not want them. You must believe in yourself, because you *can* accomplish your goals. Set your standards high. Work hard. Stay optimistic, and don't give up, even when life gets tough.

John A. Garrison

TABLE OF CONTENTS

ACKNOWLEDGMENTS

Thank you to Sharon Kizziah-Holmes for making the book publishing business a pleasant process. Thank you to Velvet Fackeldey for keen-eyed editing. Thanks to numerous writer friends who made suggestions for manuscript refinements, for listening and commiserating when I was stuck on a portion, and who celebrated when I announced the manuscript had gone to press. And of course, thank you to John A. Garrison for selecting me to tell his story.

PROLOGUE

◆

February winds howling across the northern Missouri prairie couldn't drown the cries of a woman giving birth.

The doctor wiped his brow on his shoulder just before the woman's last scream, and delivered the thin baby. Wind whistled through cracks in the walls of the rickety farm house, not much more than a shack. "You've got a boy, Mrs. Garrison."

"Boy. Girl. One too many," she whispered.

"He's healthy, if a bit small. Here you go." The doctor wrapped a threadbare blanket around the baby and laid him on his mother's chest. She said no words of thanks, but unwrapped the baby to look at hands, toes, tiny body.

The doctor spoke softly as he wrote in the family bible, "Let's see. It's the fourth of February, nineteen thirty-three." He barely heard the woman say, "I'm forty-two years old. Don't need another baby. Russell will see to your pay. Please send Margaret in. I, I -" Her voice faded.

CHAPTER ONE

◆

When I was eleven years old, my parents gave me to neighbors where I worked for my room and meals.

CHAPTER TWO

Making my first million was the hardest. The rest came much easier.

CHAPTER THREE

◆

I was ten years old before my parents got an official state of Missouri birth certificate, and only then because they had to prove my age to get some sort of welfare. I think they'd signed up for government commodities—flour, sugar, cheese—that sort of thing.

My sister Margaret had to pick up the things in town, bring them to the farm on the school bus. She rode the bus from our farm to Winston for high school. We didn't have a car. It was four miles to town, too far to walk. She said it was humiliating, bringing welfare food home on the school bus.

I could imagine. I didn't ride the bus. Alta Vista one-room school was only a quarter mile away and I went there. Walked.

Mom was 42 when I was born. She once told me I should have been stillborn. I don't know why a mother would say that. Two of her children died before I was born. One daughter lived, my sister

Margaret.

Someone once told me I was a change of life baby. I guess they meant my mother was worn out with caring for kids, seeing two die—and watching the man she married turn into a mean, lyin' son-of-a-gun years before I came along.

My oldest sister, Virginia, died in 1935 at the birth of her own third child. Virginia was married with two kids way before I was born. I was only two when she passed so have no memory of her. Her husband and kids didn't come visit us so they've always been strangers to me.

I never knew my brother, either. He died at age seventeen, five years before my unwanted entry into the world. His name was Omar Russell Garrison. Omar died of a ruptured appendix.

More than once, Mom said Omar had been wonderful and I was nothing but trouble. Both my parents compared me to him over and over and I never measured up. Not once. That was no way to encourage a kid, but they didn't know—or didn't care.

My sister who lived was named Margaret Juanita. She was nine and a half years older than me. We got along as far as you could in a family that didn't talk much. She was fourteen and in high school when I started first grade. She helped me some with homework.

Both parents cared for Margaret way more than for me. I didn't hold that against her. It wasn't her fault. She would tease me some, but it wasn't mean. One time a big storm was coming and mom got us kids into the cellar. It was one of those outside things, with a door that was almost flat to the ground. The cellar walls were made from rough Missouri rocks. Mom stored her home-canned goods down there. She'd made shelves to line the cellar walls so we were surrounded by glass jars of green beans, tomatoes, and applesauce.

It was a rip roaring storm, but no tornado. We hunkered down and waited for it to pass. Mom kept a kerosene lamp in the cellar and it flickered as gusts of wind puffed through cracks in the old door. The storm was so loud you couldn't talk. After it got quiet, we knew the storm had blown over so we climbed out of the cellar and headed back to the house. We couldn't get in. Somehow the doors got locked and we didn't have a key. We went around the house and tried all the windows. Down tight except for a little one in the pantry closet off the kitchen.

"Come here, John. You're the only one who can fit through the window. You can crawl through and come open the door for Margaret and me." Mom was going to push me through the little window.

That seemed like fun so I got ready for a boost up. Mom took hold of me just as my sister said, "What if there's a booger man inside?"

A booger man? I squirmed out of Mom's grasp. I wasn't going through that window to face a booger man! She tried to catch me, told me my sister was just teasing. But I wasn't hearing Mom. Margaret knew and I trusted her. I didn't trust Mom.

I don't remember how we finally got into the house.

CHAPTER FOUR

We never had much in the way of birthday celebrations at our house, not for anyone. But I do remember one February fourth we had homemade ice cream and Mom said it was my birthday. I'd cut the ice on the pond so the old crank freezer had ice and for a change, we had milk, cream and sugar. It made me shiver but it tasted real good. Another time I had some tinker toys but those might have come from an uncle or aunt. All my grandparents died before I was born.

I don't know why my dad never had a kind word for me. And often as not, instead of talk, he'd knock me around—or try to. I was seven or eight and not very tall but pretty strong from farm work when I started defending myself by dodging out of his reach, or by throwing a rock back at him. He'd get even madder so I'd take off and lay low in the woods until I could sneak back to the house and hang around my mom. He didn't hit me so hard around her.

Dad shoved my mom around some, but don't think he hit her with his hands or fists. His words did, but not his hands. They had many loud arguments.

My full name is John Anderson Garrison. My father was Russell Garrison and his dad was Anderson Hall Garrison. I'm glad my name reflects my grandpa more than my dad. My grandpa did all right by his family as far as I know, but on a northern Missouri farm before and during the Great Depression, life was hard. Even so, he was a better person than the one son who managed to become my dad.

Dad was next to the youngest of twelve children. He never got along very well with his brothers and sisters. Something just wasn't right about that man. He never figured out you get more out of people when you're nice instead of mean.

CHAPTER FIVE

◆

Russell Garrison—Dad—was a poor money manager with what little he had, and when he didn't have money in the bank, he wrote checks anyway. Seemed like someone was always after him and we lived in fear of him going to jail, and then it would be even worse for the family.

My earliest memory of my dad being in trouble happened when I was around four years old. We lived on a farm Dad rented or maybe sharecropped—hard to say what the deal was.

The house was a two-story shack, like a lot of farm houses all over the country after the Great Depression. It had holes in the walls and a ground hog had a den underneath it. We dodged the critter for three or four days inside the house until it realized we weren't going away so it left.

The house was cold in the winter and hot in the summer but winter was the worst time. Margaret and I had tiny rooms upstairs. We slept on cots. You couldn't get warm under a couple of thin quilts, even with your clothes and socks on. I'd curl up under those old quilts and shiver myself to sleep.

Those old houses didn't have any insulation so didn't hold heat. There was a wood cook stove in the kitchen and a small pot-bellied stove in the front room. Once the wood finished burning up each night, it was colder than sin in the house. A bucket of water on the stove would be frozen by morning.

All winter the wind howled and whistled through those holes in the wall and snow drifted inside. My parents slept in a squeaky old bed downstairs, where it was warmer.

Summers weren't so bad at night because we'd open all the windows and get a little ventilation. Even upstairs, the house smelled of grease and mold. Old wallpaper had been stuck up with flour and water paste. Mice chewed on it year-round.

That part of northern Missouri is flat so you could see the dust from a car coming down those gravel roads a long, long way off. Even going slow, a car would stir up a trail of dust that bloomed up in the air like a moving, ugly cloud. You'd stop whatever you were doing and try to figure out who the car belonged to— the neighbor, or a traveling salesman, or maybe a preacher trying to drum up business for a revival meeting.

We were working in the garden one hot, dry summer day when we heard the sounds of a car way off in the distance. I was pulling weeds alongside my sister. Mom was hoeing. Everyone stopped what they were doing and looked toward the road. Dad made a squinty face. I hoped it meant we could go inside out of the hot sun and maybe have some lemonade, but I could tell right off that wouldn't happen. Dad got all nervous acting and stared hard at the dust trail until he could see a big black car - no one he or Mom recognized. He mumbled something like, "Oh law! I've got to get outta here." He took off running across the field towards the woods behind the house.

Mom dropped her hoe and hustled Margaret and me into the house. We waited for the car to turn into our driveway, which was about a half mile or so of dirt path off the county's graveled road. Mom wiped her hands on her apron and muttered. She figured it was the law looking for my dad for another bad check. She fussed and fumed. I held onto her apron and kept quiet.

We could hear the car getting close. Mom pulled back the curtain just a little and looked out the front room window. My sister went into the kitchen. I peeked around Mom and saw the car, a big black, shiny thing, go past our driveway and on down the road.

Mom let out her breath in a big puff. She said, "Well I'll be. Just someone out doing their business. No one to bother us and now Russell's gone. Well, that's left us in a pickle. Again."

CHAPTER SIX

◆

After my dad took off, we were in a bad way—no way to earn a living. We didn't have a telephone or a car, so mom wrote letters to her relatives and asked for help. Her brother, Henry Kirchner, drove out from Kansas City to see us. The grownups talked at the kitchen table. Margaret and I got sent outside.

My mom, my sister and I moved to Uncle Henry's farm. He lived and worked in Kansas City so the farm house sat vacant.

The house wasn't anything grand, but better than what we left behind. We had a house without holes to let in snow. We had a barn, too, and even had a cow so we kids got to drink milk at breakfast and supper. Mom made butter, and sometimes in the summer she made cottage cheese. She did something with the milk to make it start curdling, then she wrapped the stuff in cheesecloth and hung it on the clothesline. She put a bucket underneath to catch the whitish-blue drip. Buttermilk. We drank that, too, or Mom used it to make pancakes and biscuits.

The house had a well with a pump and a bucket. It was good water. And the outhouse was down a long path behind the house. I'd watch out for snakes along the path—and in the outhouse, too.

Only thing about Uncle Henry's farm I didn't care for was a lot of snakes. It had black snakes, blue racers, spread heads and garter snakes. Never saw any rattlers, though. Thank goodness for that. But those blacksnakes would get in the rafters of the barn or overhead in the outhouse. Don't know what they'd be looking for up there other than mice.

Sometimes a snake would get into the house. The house had mice and snakes liked to go after them. The snake sometimes made its way up the walls and into either my or Margaret's room. The floors upstairs were dried out and warped and had some big cracks. Mom would kill the snakes.

In early spring, Mom ordered baby chickens from a catalog and the mail man delivered them. There must have been 500. She raised enough chickens to have eggs to sell for grocery money. She'd butcher the young roosters and some of the hens before they got big enough to be egg-layin' and sold some of the full-grown chickens, too.

They were free range chickens that came inside a shed to roost at night. Mom shut the chicken shed door tight to protect them from foxes, coyotes, and stray dogs.

CHAPTER SEVEN

◆

It was wonderful relief without my dad hitting on me and calling me names. I hoped he was gone for good. I know it was hard for Mom, though, living out in the country with two kids. She didn't have kind words or a soft touch for me, but she didn't hit me with her fist or a board so that was a welcome relief.

Uncle Henry and Aunt Elsie Kirchner came to visit every two or three weeks. Their daughter, Dorothy, came with them a time or two. She didn't talk much. Dorothy was a year or two older than my sister Margaret. Dorothy soon got married and went out on her own.

Friends from Kansas City came with my uncle and aunt sometimes. One man had a big red dog. The man gave the dog pieces of baloney. Good baloney just thrown to the dog! That baloney looked mighty tasty and when the grownups weren't looking, I tried to get some away from the dog, but he wouldn't share. He growled and I backed off. I knew better than to ask the man for a piece—Mom wouldn't have liked that. Didn't seem like good manners to me when the man gave the dog good baloney. He must have noticed me looking at it all hungry like.

Mom may have been on welfare. She didn't have anything to sell to make money other than the chickens and in the winter they didn't lay many eggs. She'd have a big garden like everybody back then. She'd can vegetables and sometimes she canned beef to eat in the winter. Jars of canned food lined the cellar walls.

We got Montgomery Ward catalogs in the mail and when Mom could afford it, she'd order us school clothes. The old catalogs went in the outhouse where we'd rip out pages to use for toilet paper.

Out back of the house there was a well and a bucket where we got our water. We kept a dipper tied up on a piece of binder twine. It wasn't the old style bucket with a bail-type handle. The new one was about three feet long and about 5 inches in diameter. It was easier to maneuver than the old style bucket and held more water. If you were strong enough to pull up the bucket with the rope and pulley system, you could get a drink any time you wanted.

We had enough food most of the time, but our clothes were sometimes little more than rags. Clothes got mended and worn 'til there were holes in elbows and knees. I had a couple of chambray shirts for summer and a pair of blue denim overalls. In winter I wore long sleeved flannel shirts and underwear called a Union suit with a trap door for doing your outhouse business. We kept wearing the same things until they completely fell apart or got too small. When the soles of our shoes started to come off, we tied them together with binder twine until even that couldn't hold them in place.

One day Mom called me aside. "John, you're starting school tomorrow. Here's things you'll need and don't you dare waste them. No money for replacements. Everyone at school has to bring a tablet and pencil. You'll get books at the school."

She handed me a big red tablet and a big thick pencil. The tablet had a picture of an Indian in a headdress on the front. The pages all had lines on them. I sniffed the paper. Loved the smell. I looked at Mom.

"Keep that tablet and pencil safe in your room tonight. Right after breakfast tomorrow you'll walk to Alta Vista school. School is important. You need to do good work there, mind the teacher."

She gave Margaret a blue cloth notebook with white loose loaf paper inside. She also gave Margaret a skinny yellow pencil and an ink pen. Margaret would start high school the next day.

Alta Vista was a one-room school with about fifteen kids spread out over grades one through eight. I had to walk about a half mile to get there and carried my lunch in a brown paper bag. I learned my letters and my numbers at Alta Vista. I liked numbers—took to arithmetic right off. I liked recess time, too. We played softball and tag, the girls right along with the boys.

My sister started high school as I started first

grade. The high school was in town so she rode a school bus to get there.

CHAPTER EIGHT

Uncle Henry's farm had a creek that ran during the spring and early summer when it rained a lot. It was great, having a creek. When it got hot in the summer and the creek started to dwindle, I'd dig holes to deepen pools of water and trap fish. I'd put a bucket in the hole and sometimes blue gill would swim into it. I'd hoist up the bucket and take the fish back to the house for Mom to fry.

Three or four little fish made us a good meal, especially if mom baked cornbread to go with it. Mom wouldn't let us drink milk, only water when we had fish for a meal.

One time, when the creek was running good in early summer, I went fishing with a cane pole and fishing hook I'd found in the barn. I'd dug up some earth worms for bait and threaded one on the hook and went walking down the creek, looking for a deep spot that might have some fish in it. I came across a little waterfall with about three feet of drop and a good sized pool. It looked real promising so I dropped my hook and waited for a tug on the line. I waited and waited, still as could be. All of a sudden I felt a big tug and I yanked that line out of the water. Wouldn't you know there was a snake on the line! I threw down my pole and ran to save my life. It was well known that water moccasins were the meanest kind of snake and could kill you with their bite and it was a terrible, painful way to die.

I didn't tell my mom about the snake. Later, I went back real careful and saw the snake had gotten away so I grabbed my fishing pole and ran back to the barn.

After that I focused on trapping rabbits. A neighbor boy, J.L. Davis, taught me how to make a rabbit trap. The trap was made of boards. We hammered together a rectangular box and J.L. fastened a trap door that we blocked up with a stick. We'd bait the trap with a piece of lettuce or carrot and leave the trap in the edge of the woods. Next day we'd go check it and if we'd caught a rabbit, we'd work together to not let it escape. I'd slowly pull up the trap door and when it tried to run out, J.L. would hit it and kill it. Then we'd skin it, gut it, and take the meat to the house for a tasty meal of fried rabbit.

J.L. saved the pelts. He knew how to clean them up, and then he'd sell them in town. People liked to carry a lucky rabbit's foot in those days. It was a dried up foot – a real rabbit foot attached to a little key chain you carried in your pocket. You'd buy them in the Five and Dime Store. If you were lucky, you had a pocket knife hooked onto the chain.

J.L. taught me to hunt, too. His dad had a single-shot .22 rifle he'd let us use. In those days, you didn't dare waste bullets so you learned to hit the rabbit on a hop and nail him with the first try. Getting a jack rabbit was better than a cottontail because they were bigger. More meat on the bones. Jack rabbits would run in a straight line so it was easier to shoot them. Cotton tails would zig-zag so they made a harder target, trying to time their hop so you didn't waste a bullet.

Sometimes Mom went to church and took me with her. In summers the churches had revivals, meetings every night for one week. They'd bring in special preachers to do revival services.

This one time the preacher said we should all come back the next night to see something they'd never see again. We wondered what on earth that might be. Went back the next night to find out. Just in case it was something scary, we sat in the back row.

The service went on and on, one hymn after another, and lots of praying and talking. I tried not to fidget. Finally, the special preacher got up and told us we were going to see something we'd never see again. He had a bag in his hand and held it up for everyone to see. I sat up tall as I could and held my breath. The whole congregation sat up straight as could be and got real quiet.

You couldn't hear a sound except the "whoosh" of people fanning themselves. The preacher put his hand in the bag, pulled out a peanut, cracked it, and ate it. Everyone laughed.

Dad eventually got word the law wasn't after him and came back. Either he'd written to Mom or asked around and found us at Uncle Henry's place. I was sad when Mom let him move in. The two years he was gone were blessed relief for me. Maybe she thought he'd learned his lesson. He hadn't.

CHAPTER NINE

◆

Most people have pictures of themselves and their families as a child. I don't. Don't think my folks owned a camera. My grandparents both died before I was born and we didn't get many visits from aunts or uncles. You'd think someone would have a picture of me, but the only one I have is a group school picture during my second grade. I'm grinning big in the picture because it was more fun to be in school than at home.

As a kid, I most always had a smile on my face. Sometimes that got me in trouble.

One time a teacher whacked me with a ruler because I was grinning at the wrong time. The teacher stood at the chalk board and put an arithmetic problem down. Then turned to the class and started to talk. Arithmetic was easy for me and I saw the answer right off, so I grinned. He thought I was making fun of him and didn't give me a chance to explain. Called me a smart mouth. Told me to wipe the grin off my face.

Another time I got in trouble at school I got called a thief.

I had a mechanical pencil called an Ever Sharp. I'd used up my lead and saw a piece on the floor by the teacher's desk. I waited until his back was turned to the chalk board and I reached for the lead. He turned around and caught me.

"John Garrison, what do you think you're doing?"

"Well, sir, I was tryin' to get some lead that fell out of my pencil."

"That lead didn't fall out of your pencil and you know it! It fell off my desk. You've got no call to be grinning. You're a thief."

The whole class stared at me. I didn't say anything.

"Come up here."

I had no choice but to drag my heels up to the teacher. I figured he'd make me apologize. Embarrass me in front of the class some more. They knew I was poor and didn't have money to buy lead for my pencil. But he grabbed his ruler, spun me around and said, "Bend over!"

He whacked my behind with that ruler in the front of the classroom with everyone watching. That scene got the rest of the class to pay attention but didn't help my attitude. I didn't really think about smiling, it was just part of how I looked like hair color and eyes and nose. It was just there. It still is.

My dad tried to slap the smile off of my face more than once.

On the farm, if I wasn't working fast enough, Dad would throw rocks at me and once he threw a hammer. I started fighting back, throwing stuff back at him. That really made him mad but I felt I had to defend myself. I'd throw whatever he threw back at him, and then I'd take off to the woods for a few hours until he calmed down.

CHAPTER TEN

We had good neighbors at Uncle Henry's farm. One neighbor gave me a dog I named Brownie. He'd go hunting with me. He'd tree a squirrel and while the critter was hiding from the dog on one side of the tree, I'd sidle around to the other side and throw a rock and knock the squirrel out of the tree. Kill it. I'd take it home for Mom to cook. She'd fry it and make gravy with the drippings. That was mighty fine eating. Almost as good as rabbit, but the squirrels were smaller so you didn't get as much to eat.

One day Dad was working on the hay wagon and I criticized something he did—saw an easier way to do what he was trying to do.

"Why you-," He lunged toward me. I'd seen that move many times before and dodged. He grabbed a stick and swung at me. He didn't hear Brownie growl. But he felt it when Brownie's teeth clamped onto his calf. Overalls didn't stop the pressure of the dog's jaws.

"Sic 'um Brownie!" I said. Brownie did.

Dad whacked at Brownie with the stick. Brownie yelped and took off. Dad ran after him but didn't go far. I took off, too—the opposite side of the barn from Dad.

"C'mon Brownie!" I high tailed it to the woods. Brownie beat me there, of course. In the edge of the woods I stopped long enough to make sure Dad had given up the chase. He was limping back toward the house. I took a deep breath.

We stayed in the woods until sun down. I sneaked to the house and hung out by my mom. Dad wouldn't whale on me around her—not as hard, anyway. Brownie went to the barn. He'd bed down in the straw there.

As he got older, Brownie started going off on rambles by himself. One day dad said, "Neighbor caught Brownie chasing their cows. Can't have that! I had to shoot that worthless dog."

I hated him even more.

Dad came up with different schemes for making money and saving himself work. He talked a neighbor into renting some of our pasture to have more grazing for his cows. Only thing, he didn't check with Uncle Henry, who'd planned to bale hay from the pasture. Dad couldn't pay what the hay would have brought. He and Mom argued.

I never heard him say what he did with the money. Never saw him drunk but he could've sneaked to town for a bender.

Uncle Henry was furious. He told us to clear out so we had to move again right quick.

Then there was the problem of our cows. Dad hadn't bought the cows. He rented them from a dairy. He paid rent on the cows each month from money he got selling the milk. He found a farm to rent near Cameron and moved the cows. He made me go with him. He didn't have enough money to rent the house, so we lived in the barn. Mom and Margaret were still welcome to stay at Uncle Henry's house.

I hadn't realized things could be worse than living in the same house with him, but living in that barn was worse than awful. We ate meals at the farmer's but had to sleep in the barn, wash up with a bucket of cold water from the well.

Dad worked for the farmer milking cows and doing other chores. He tended to his own rental cows in the early morning and late evening. I had to help milk, too. Once I wasn't doing it to suit dad and he took after me. I saw him jump toward me and I took off. Don't think he even tried to catch me because I could run faster than him for a while. I made my way through the pasture, down the gravel road to the state highway. Started walking back to Uncle Henry's farm where mom and Margaret still lived.

The state highway was a two-lane blacktopped road. A couple of cars passed and I kept walking. Then I heard a car slow and I glanced over. It was a state trooper. He pulled over to the side and got out. I stood still.

"Hello there, young fellow." The trooper smiled at me.

"Hello." I tried to smile.

"How come you're walking all by yourself?"

"I'm going home."

"Need a lift?"

When I hesitated, he said, "You're not in trouble. I'm glad to give you a ride home."

"Yes, sir. If you don't mind. It's a ways." I'd relaxed when he said I wasn't in trouble. Didn't tell him about my mean dad and him making me live in a barn.

The trooper drove me the twelve or fourteen miles toward home. We'd gone down the gravel road toward the house about a mile and had to stop. The creek had gotten up about a hundred yards from the house. It was too deep across the low water bridge to drive the car.

"I'm going to have to turn around here. Any way for you to get to the house?"

"Yes sir. I know where the creek gets shallow at the end of that pasture."

"All right then. You be careful."

"I will. Thank you for the ride. I'm glad to be home."

I crawled under a fence and walked downstream until I could find a place to cross. I made my way over to the house and went in the kitchen door.

Mom didn't say anything—didn't tell me I had to go back. So I got to stay. I had to help her on the farm but anything was better than living with my dad's temper and that old barn.

CHAPTER ELEVEN

◆

Dad eventually got enough money together to rent the house and bring Mom and me there. Lucky for my sister, she moved to Kansas City soon as she finished high school. She worked as a house keeper for some people.

When Margaret came to visit, she brought me candy bars! Sometimes she'd bring me new clothes and those were nice, but I liked the candy best.

Dad messed up again. He got behind on the rent for the cows and the milk company repossessed them.

We moved to an eighty acre farm he bought with help from his sister Kate and her husband. Aunt Kate and her husband lived near Omaha, Nebraska so they didn't know how bad a business person my dad was. The old house had been vacant for years. It was a mess. We moved in and cleaned it up best we could.

The house had five rooms, one story. We had

kerosene lights in the house and a kerosene lantern to carry outside to the barn. No one who lived in the country back then had electricity. Our cook stove was fueled by wood and we had a pot-bellied stove in the living room for heat.

We'd moved kind of late in the year for cutting wood and besides, Dad didn't like sawing down trees and making firewood. He never liked hard work. So we didn't have hardly any wood to burn that winter and the house never got warm. When Mom had fire in the cook stove, I'd hunker down behind it to keep warm as I could until bed time.

One Christmas we had a tree—a cedar I'd cut. Mom hung some tinsel and a few ornaments on it. I got tinker toys for a gift. Only time I remember getting a gift at Christmas.

My dad kept on being mean to me and as I got bigger, I fought back even more. One time he threw a pitch fork at me and it stuck between my sock and my shoe. I guess I was lucky it didn't hit me higher up. Could have killed me. I was ten years old.

Mom always insisted I go to school, so when we lived there, I went to Gallatin. I walked a quarter mile down our lane to the road and caught the yellow school bus. It was the first time I'd ridden a bus to school. It was an old '37 Chevrolet. Neighbors named Townsends had eight kids who also rode the bus—four girls and four boys. It was about twelve miles to Gallatin.

In the Gallatin school each grade had their own teacher! We had a lunch hour. You could buy lunch there, or bring your own lunch, or go up town to buy lunch. I liked going uptown. There was a little store about two blocks from school that sold crackers and bologna. We'd eat in back by the pot-bellied stove. Sometimes I'd spend my quarter for lunch on a quart of ice cream - strawberry, vanilla, or butter brickle. Didn't like chocolate so much. Sometimes Richard Kirchberger went with me so he could smoke. I tried smoking but didn't like the taste.

I went to fourth, fifth, and sixth grade at Gallatin.

CHAPTER TWELVE

◆

One of our neighbors, Mr. Foley, raised sheep. He was a great neighbor—talked with me. Didn't yell at me. He gave me lambs his ewes rejected. See, when a ewe had triplets she would only accept two. Mr. Townsend gave me the third one to bottle feed—showed me how. If I could keep it alive, I'd raise it big enough to sell wool. Eventually, I'd sell the sheep. I'd have to keep the newborn lambs in the house, and Mom said that was okay. When big enough, I'd put the lambs in the barn. When weaned off the bottle, they went into a pasture.

One time I had accumulated six sheep and the wool I sold brought ten dollars. That was a lot of money for me. I slept with my money under my pillow. On Saturday morning I walked twelve miles to town and bought a battery operated radio. It was a heavy thing and I had to stop and rest several times, but eventually made it back home.

Everyone listened to my radio. We could tune it in and get the Lone Ranger and Captain Midnight shows. Those were wonderful shows. That was the best times we had as a family with everyone sitting quiet, listening to my radio.

I should have known it was too good to last.

One day while I was at school, dad sold all my sheep. I put up a huge fuss – said he'd stolen them and kept my money I'd been saving up to buy a bicycle. My mother said the money wasn't stolen, it was in the bank. I knew what that meant—dad would write a check and my money would be gone.

I told Mr. Foley what my dad had done. He said if the money was in the bank, then I could write a check before my dad did. He explained a counter check. In those days, all the stores had blank checks at the cash register. You could print the name of your bank on top, write your check, sign your name, and it was good as having money in your pocket.

Determined to get my bicycle, I walked to town.

The man who owned the hardware store had a used bicycle. As if I'd done it every day, I wrote a check for it and signed my mother's name.

I started to ride the bicycle home. Only thing, riding a bicycle turned out to be much harder than I'd imagined, especially on gravel. Falling on gravel hurts a lot. I walked most of the twelve miles back to our farm. When I got close, I checked to make sure no one could see me and hid the bicycle in a shed we didn't use much.

Eventually, I learned to ride my bicycle.

When the bank statement arrived, the jig was up. They saw a check written for $25 to the hardware store. Neither of them wrote the check so

I got nailed. Both parents lit into me. The checking account was in my mother's name only, although dad sold the sheep and made the deposit. After lots of shouting and me dodging dad's fists, I got away. I went to the Foleys to lay low until things cooled off at my house.

While I was gone, my parents called social services.

Next day, a strange car rolled up our driveway. A young woman got out and Mom welcomed her like she'd known her before. The woman was a social worker. She was nice. She took me for a walk down the lane and talked to me.

"John, your parents think it best for you to go stay with someone else for a while. I've talked with another farm family that would like to have you. You'll stay with them, do farm chores there, go to school. Do you understand?"

I nodded my head. I understood my parents were getting rid of me. Wished I could go to Kansas City like Margaret but no one made the offer.

"I'll drive you over there tomorrow. Pack your things tonight. Okay?"

I nodded again. "I'm taking my bicycle."

"All right. I think the bicycle will fit in my car trunk. I'll see you tomorrow."

That evening, I overheard talk. Dad wanted to put me in the detention home at Booneville but the social worker had said I didn't qualify. I hadn't really broken any laws by writing the check. But both parents wanted me out of the house at that point. Instead, of juvenile detention, they put me in foster care. I don't know what all paperwork it took, but they got rid of me.

I landed at a farm near Jamesport, Missouri with a family named Teeter. I was eleven years old.

CHAPTER THIRTEEN

◆

At the Teeter's farm I worked hard as a grown hired hand. They had me up early morning to work, up late each evening and every weekend. I went to a one-room country school. There were only about a dozen kids there. Going to school was required by Social Services or I'm sure I'd not have gone.

Mrs. Teeter treated me like an unwanted body to feed, but that wasn't much different from what I'd had at home. I had meals and a bed. Breakfast was usually a bowl of oatmeal, and then I rode my bicycle to school. After school I did whatever chores Mr. Teeter had for me—milking, hauling manure, chopping wood—then we ate supper. After supper I went to bed.

No toys, no books, no radio. Nothing but my thoughts.

I vowed to never be poor when I grew up.

Only thing I liked there was driving their new Ferguson tractor. It was a nice machine and I learned to plow and disc. Up on the tractor, I controlled my world. It felt good.

Old Man Teeter was mean. He didn't throw rocks at me but he wasn't nice, either. One time he didn't like how I was milking. He grabbed me and shook me hard—yanked my clothes half off. I put myself back together best I could and finished milking. I hated that man. Felt like a prisoner.

A few days later Old Teeter caught a stray dog and fastened a rag to the dog's tail with a piece of baling wire. He lit the rag. I wanted to cry for the poor dog. The thing ran off but managed to get into the barn and set it afire. The barn burned down and the dog got away. I thought that was justice, the barn burning.

On weekends the Teeters would go to Mrs. Teeter's relatives the other side of Jamesport. They took me with them. Probably didn't trust me at home alone. One time they took along a neighbor boy who was several years older, maybe seventeen. They got up a game of softball. The older boy pitched and Mr. Teeter hit the balls. They made me chase the balls and bring them back to the pitcher. I was short and kind of stocky. They made fun of how I ran. Acted as if I couldn't hear. I'd have lit into them if I was bigger.

When they got tired of the game and went into the house, I hung around outside, pretending to play catch with myself. Soon as they got inside, I sneaked off. On the county road, a good blacktopped road with a fair amount on traffic. I caught a ride back to my folks' place. They weren't happy to see me but I went to my room and shut the door.

I was there only a couple of hours when the Teeters came and got me.

After that, things went from bad to worse. Both the Teeters talked even meaner to me. And no matter what anyone says, words hurt. After a couple weeks, I sneaked off and went home again. The Teeters came after me.

"No, I'm not going back there. You can't make me. That man is mean! He hit me and called me names. I'll tell the law." I ran to the barn, out the door and into the woods. Waited until it was almost dark before going back to the house.

My parents didn't make me go that time.

After several days, the social worker brought back my bicycle and my cardboard box of clothes.

CHAPTER FOURTEEN

My parents sold the eighty acre farm at Gallatin and bought forty acres south of Hamilton. Don't know why the new place was smaller. Must have been better farm land and less woods.

There, I went to New York Consolidated school. It wasn't as big as Gallatin but a good school. It was two stories and no more than two grades in each room. I finished sixth and seventh grades there.

Dad took off again. Don't know what happened but when I got home from school one day he was gone. I was glad, except Mom was in a pickle. She had to find work.

Mom found a job taking care of an elderly woman in Dockery, a tiny place near Richmond, Missouri. Only thing, it was too far to walk from our place so she lived at the woman's house. I would have been on my own and she wouldn't have that. Instead, I went to live with a cousin of Dad's named Vern Duffey. He lived northwest of Galatin,

Missouri about thirty miles from where Mom worked.

Cousin Vern had no children at home so he wanted me to help with farm work. I did. Gladly. The Duffeys were nice to me. In fact, it turned out to be the nicest place I ever lived until I was grown and on my own.

Vern's wife, Florence, was sickly and spent a lot of time in bed with headaches, likely some type of migraine. The country doctor couldn't do much for her, only tell her to rest. She'd close the curtains and take to bed with a wet cloth over her eyes when she felt a headache coming on.

Vern did most of the cooking and cleaning as well as the farm chores. I helped with chores inside and outside the house and even learned to cook some. I carried in wood, helped feed his livestock. He had beef cattle except for one milk cow. Guess he thought I milked just fine because he never yelled at how I milked or how I did any work. He'd just show me what he needed done. I appreciated Vern more than I ever could say.

The Duffy's farm was too far out of Gallatin for the school bus, so I went to Spring Hill School. It was another one-room school. There were three of us in eighth grade. I lived with Vern and Florence all school year and the start of summer.

At time for my graduation from eighth grade, my mother somehow came up with money for a pair of dress pants and a good shirt for me. She managed money way better than my dad ever could. She'd have been better off without him a long time before far as I could see.

That summer I stayed on at the Duffy's and got a job as the hired hand for a neighbor named Ernest Allen. My dad had worked for him and didn't have too much to say about the man, so I figured he'd be an honorable employer. I was wrong.

Ernest Allen owned almost seven hundred acres and needed lots of help. I rode my bike to work, and back to the Duffeys each evening. I helped Vern with his chores, ate supper with them, slept there. I really liked working for money, even though Allen was hated by all the neighbors. If a neighbor's cow got through the fence onto his property, he'd keep the cow, that sort of thing. It was theft, but somehow the law never did anything about him. Since farmers didn't brand their cattle, it would be the neighbor's word against his, and people pretty much followed "live and let live" and just avoided Allen much as they could.

Allen was mean to me in a different way from anyone else before or since. One day he grabbed me. Abused me sexually.

I got away and went back to the Duffeys. I told Vern just a little, gathered my things, and rode my bicycle back to my parents' farm. My bicycle had a carryall over the back tire and I put the cardboard box of my things there and rode home. It was about thirty miles of gravel and blacktop highway. Had to stop and rest a few times, but I made it.

There was no place for me to go to high school, except Hamilton. It was four and a half miles and I could have ridden my bicycle each day. J.C. Penney had made his money and built a high school for his home town. Only thing, I really liked working for money and didn't have a job in Hamilton, so my formal schooling ended at eighth grade. I decided it was time to go someplace else. I had to find a job.

I had worked for Allen three months and had fifty dollars saved.

My sister had finished high school and was working for Montgomery Ward in Kansas City. I could probably have asked her for help, but she'd have insisted I go to high school. I wanted to find a job and be a grownup.

My dad had talked a lot about Denver and the days he worked there as a young man. It sounded like a wonderful place, way better than Northern Missouri. He made it sound like jobs were plentiful and everyone was friendly. I packed my clothes into a cardboard box and bought a train ticket to Denver, Colorado.

I was thirteen.

CHAPTER FIFTEEN

◆

It was a long, hot ride from Hamilton, Missouri to Denver, Colorado. I watched the flat, flat, landscape all through Kansas and Eastern Colorado. Didn't have any reading materials. Don't remember if I bought anything to eat on the train—must have, somehow. The train rocked and rumbled and I hung onto my seat. I slept in my seat, woke, figured out there was a bathroom and managed to use it, then and went back to my seat.

I got off the train in Denver and looked this way and that. It didn't look anything like I'd pictured from my dad's glowing stories. I started walking up and down streets. It was a huge, noisy, busy city—a tough place for a thirteen year old country boy. I walked and walked. Finally found a flea bag cheap hotel. Got some strange looks from the desk clerk, but he sold me a room for a couple nights.

Only thing Dad said was true about Denver and Colorado was the mountains. They were huge.

Spectacular.

The only job I could find was washing pots and pans in a café kitchen. It was hot as a firecracker in that kitchen. After a couple hours I got sick and had to go outside to keep from passing out. After two days, I got told to move on.

There was an outdoor market close to my hotel and I walked around there.

"Hey there, young fellow. What can I do for you?" A man selling vegetables smiled at me. "Want to buy anything."

"No thank you. I'm looking for a job."

"Looking for a job? Wish I could help you out but I don't know anyone looking to hire. What kind of skills do you have?" The vegetable man looked me up and down but kept smiling.

"I know how to do lots of things. I can wash dishes. I can tend sheep. Ride a horse. Milk cows."

"Then you might do best to hitch a ride up into ranching country. I hear they're always looking for help."

"How do I get there?"

"Go north into Wyoming. They have cattle and sheep ranches both up there. Go down this street 'til you get to the edge of town, stand on the side of the road and stick your thumb out."

"I believe I'll do that. Don't much like washing dishes in a hot kitchen. Thank you."

I'd learned to ride a horse on one of my farm jobs, so I figured ranching would do. I'd be a cowboy.

It was 1946, the war was over and lots of people had cars. The spirit in the country was high—people were in good moods. I hitched rides with decent people all the way to Saratoga, Wyoming. Besides, a kid with a small cardboard box for a suitcase couldn't have anything worth stealing.

Saratoga only had about a thousand people and everyone seemed to know everyone else. It had hot springs, a tourist attraction, but I couldn't afford the hotel there. I found a cheap hotel, paid for a room, and asked the owner if he knew of anyone looking for help. He said he didn't but he'd ask his son. The owner's son knew several farmers and ranchers. He told me about a family looking for help and said he'd telephone that ranch.

The next morning the rancher picked me up and took me out to their cattle ranch. That job saved my life. After paying for my room, I only had seventy-five cents in my pocket.

It was open range country, and each rancher was allotted so many cattle. I stayed in the bunk house with the other hired hand, an older man. He was nice enough, but didn't talk much.

We went on a cattle drive with some of the neighbors. We brought them into each ranch for the winter. I helped get the cows sorted according to the owner's brand. That was the end of my job. Someone drove me into town, paid my wages and said good-bye.

Again, I looked for work and a place to stay.

I met the son of a farmer who had sixteen acres of potatoes that needed dug. They hired me—people named Patterson. To harvest the potatoes, they had a digger pulled by horse, and a conveyer-like thing.

The owner's son and I picked up the potatoes and tossed them onto the moving conveyor. The soil was sandy and hurt my hands. The constant bending over really hurt my back but it was a job.

At the Patterson's, I stayed in the bunk house by myself. It didn't have electricity. They had a generator so the house had electric lights and a refrigerator. No one yet had electricity except in big cities.

After the Patterson's potato picking job ended, I got hired at a sheep ranch. They had around 1500 sheep and I helped to corral the sheep at night. I slept in a sheep wagon. It had a bed with lots of quilts and I kept the wagon a long ways from the ranch house. It was cold, but there were some rough men in the bunk house so I stayed away from there.

The Patterson's had a Welch pony that I used to move the wagon around. The ranch also had two dogs and they followed me around some. One day the dogs treed a porcupine. I climbed the tree, thinking I'd shoo the porcupine out of there. The porcupine turned his back, which meant he was going to throw quills at me. I let go the tree and fell to the ground hard. A stick hit me in the mouth but I didn't go crying to the ranch owner—or anyone else. Just got on with my work. Any of the ranch hands had seen me, they'd just have laughed.

I found some books at the ranch and read everything I could get my hands on. Didn't matter if it was about ranching or stories. And I saved my money.

When winter got bad, they brought the sheep inside for the duration and paid me off. I had $80 saved.

I made my way to Rawlins, Wyoming. It was a larger place so might be more jobs there. I bought an old rifle that turned out to not shoot straight. I'd thought it would be good for deer. It was only a .25/20 and as it turned out, too small to kill deer. Mistake.

I learned from each mistake. Didn't repeat.

During all the time I was out west, I didn't write to anyone. I don't know if Mom did anything to try and find where I was, but I never asked.

CHAPTER SIXTEEN

No more jobs turned up so before I ran out of money, I bought a bus ticket back to Hamilton, Missouri. The bus stopped several times and I don't remember where I slept. Had to be on a bench at a bus station, or in my seat.

I went out to my parents' farm but they were gone. Their stuff was there—furniture and bedding—but you could tell no one lived there. So I moved in. My old bicycle was there, too.

I figured Mom was still at the job north of Richmond taking care of the elderly lady. It was too far for me to ride my bicycle so one day I hitchhiked to where she worked to tell her I was back. Then I hitchhiked back to the farm.

At fourteen, I was feeling more resourceful and still didn't see the need for high school.

I did odd jobs here and there and saved as much as I could. I could eat cheap on crackers and cheese, or crackers and bologna. Mostly, I rode my bicycle for transportation. Had to do lots of tire patches, but that old bicycle took me everywhere I needed to go. In town but there was a café called the Blue Castle. They made brain sandwiches for twenty-five cents, and I'd get one of those once in a while. When I wanted to splurge, there was a café in Gallatin that sold a roast beef sandwich for twenty-five cents and a cold soda pop for five cents.

Each time I changed jobs, I made more money than at the last place.

I helped a man run a small poultry house for a dollar a day. In the summer I found a job running the reel on a combine and doubled my salary. The owner, Mr. Wilson was crippled from polio. He paid two dollars a day. But the wife there was mean. She once threw hot water on me. It was late fall and cold and I was trying to keep warm by the cook stove. She told me to move and I didn't, so she threw a teakettle of scalding hot water on me. It hit my side. I went to my room and took off my wet shirt. The skin had rolled up and it hurt bad. I put on my other shirt and laid the wet one out to dry.

The next morning, I got my bicycle and started to head out, but Mr. Wilson caught up with me and convinced me to let him put some salve on the burn. Then, he took me over to his dad's place to work. His dad had a field he wanted to get plowed.

At old man Manley Wilson's farm, I drove an F30 Farmall tractor and did all the plowing. Then I cleaned out a chicken house and a barn. But that old man didn't pay me! It was forty-two dollars I really needed, but nothing I could do. He was a big man and I was small. He knew I couldn't win. He seemed to think that giving me a few meals was enough pay.

I told my mother about the man not paying me and she borrowed a car. Together we went back to talk with that old man. He still wouldn't pay up. Don't know why other than he was cheap. We didn't go to the law. The law would have taken his side, him a respected farmer and me just a scruffy kid. They wouldn't care what my mother had to say. She was married to a ne'er-do-well man on the run from the law.

I never forgot that man. But mostly, I got along with people. Worked hard for my pay. I was getting by.

It was too good to last.

My dad came back. He talked bad about me all over town, called me an outlaw. With him back, I had to get out of there. People started thinking I might turn out like him.

I was fifteen.

CHAPTER SEVENTEEN

◆

I decided to go on the wheat harvest circuit and made my way to Fredericksburg, Oklahoma. It was May, and the harvest wouldn't be for a few months, so I looked for any kind of work I could find. I slept outside, under a truck—anywhere I could.

My money was about gone when I met an old man who needed a hired hand. He was a nice old man and his wife was nice. They let me stay in the house, fed me, helped me do my laundry. I did general farm work there like plowing and helping get ready for the fall wheat harvest. He had a Minneapolis Moline tractor that worked good. I really liked that machine.

The men who traveled across the country from Canada to Texas for the fall wheat harvest were a rough lot. The old man protected me from too many interactions with that bunch. I was still small for my age and grinned too much.

When the wheat harvest ended, I went back to

Hamilton—home, such as it was. I got in touch with my sister, Margaret. We got along better with each other than with our mother. We visited, kept up with each other's lives.

After some odd jobs, I got together enough money to buy a used Doodlebug motor scooter. That thing would go only about twenty miles per hour and was not street safe. It had six-inch wheels and no tags. I got stopped by the highway patrol a few times, warned, but didn't get any tickets. I rode the thing to Kansas one time, worked for a farmer near Lewisburg. When the job ended I went back to Missouri through Kansas City, and got into a traffic jam. Thought I'd get killed on that little scooter in the middle of all those cars.

Soon as I could, I sold the Doodlebug for $50, same amount I'd paid for it.

When I turned sixteen I went to the Five and Dime and bought a driver's license for twenty-five cents. That was before the government invented the license bureau and figured out they could get a lot of tax money there.

After I got my license I went looking for a vehicle. Needed something more than my bicycle for work. I found an old Model A pickup I could afford. That old pickup had sat in idle for a few years but I managed to get it running.

I got a job with an electrician in Richmond, about thirty miles away. My first job as an apprentice electrician was wiring a chicken hatchery. My boss and I worked together. It was simple wiring. Back then, didn't have a ground. After the hatchery, we wired some houses. When you put the wiring in those old lathe and plaster houses, you cut out one lathe and part of another so you had a place for the outlet screws. That was important to know; otherwise the socket would fall out of the wall.

He paid me $3 a day.

When veterans came back home after World War II, the government paid seventy-five percent of the vet's wages. The electrician let me go and hired a vet.

At the age of sixteen, I went out on my own as a contract electrician.

The electricity came from the Rural Electrification Administration. Everyone just called it the REA. It was part of President Roosevelt's New Deal. They'd say, "REA's coming our way. Going to get lights in the house." They came to call their electric bill "the light bill" and the electrician was "the light man."

Word about REA coming spread around the country like wild fire. Seemed like everyone wanted electricity.

The electrician didn't show me how to wire a breaker box but I figured out on my own. I asked the hardware store owner and he helped explain some things. It was an ordeal, though, and I got shocked a time or two. One time I was on an extension ladder twenty or twenty-five feet up a pole. I had my arm around a copper wire and touched a live wire. It jarred me so bad I almost fell off the pole. The power line was across the highway. I had to run the wires from the pole to the house, attach all the wires to the breaker box, and then call the electric company. They ran the wire from their pole across the highway.

As far as I know, none of the houses I wired ever burned so I guess I did all right.

CHAPTER EIGHTEEN

When I'd saved enough money I traded my old Model A pickup for a newer 1938 Chevy pickup. I bought some ladders and materials—wire, boxes, screws, and pliers. I traveled around middle and northwestern Missouri ahead of the REA people. To know where to go, I'd check where the lines were next going from headquarters in Chillocothe, Missouri. Then I'd go house to house and offer to do the wiring. Most people were excited to have electricity coming and wanted to get ready. This time, my smile did me well because people trusted me to wire their houses.

The first time, I bid low and barely paid for my materials. I did better after that and made a profit of twenty-five to thirty dollars a day. Good money. Really good money. I opened a bank account in Richmond, Missouri. Then I made a deal with a hardware store in Richmond and got a break on the price of wiring, breaker boxes, and other materials.

After each job, I'd go back to the old farm

place at night to eat and sleep. Mom still worked for the elderly lady. Still lived there.

Dad was gone again.

My sister worked in Kansas City for Montgomery Ward. We kept in touch, as family does. We visited some by telephone, and once in a while in person. But she never wanted to talk about her childhood on the various farms with Mom and Dad. And neither of us ever knew much about our aunts, uncles, cousins.

Writing those old houses was hard work. Those farm house attics were blistering hot. I wired my parents' house, donated everything. It seemed the right thing to do, even though they'd been miserable parents. Besides, it made it nicer for me living there to have lights and a place to plug in a radio.

I met a girl at a church in Dockery. It's a little town about six miles north of Richmond. She was the only girl there my age. We talked a few times but I never got the nerve to take her to a movie or anything.

Later, I met a girl from Excelsior Springs. We went roller skating. We'd also go to the park where there was a lake. I'd rent us a canoe. We went swimming some, too. One night after a movie, we lost our virginity together.

After two years, I'd wired all the houses that wanted wiring, so I needed another job. I decided to go back to Colorado.

I was eighteen.

CHAPTER NINETEEN

◆

A lot more confident than my first venture west five years earlier, I sold my pickup and bought a bus ticket to Denver.

With my work experience, I talked my way into a job at a construction company. They did contract work for the government and put me to work as a maintenance carpenter at the Rocky Mountain Arsenal. It was dangerous work. Storage bunkers in the arsenal blew up a couple times while I worked there. A guy working nights would get tired, fall asleep and something would blow. Usually that killed the guy. After those blowups, I went in to patch up and repair the place.

No flea bag hotel this time, I found an apartment in the basement of a house that was reasonably priced. An older couple owned the home. I had a hot plate to cook my meals on, and indoor plumbing. Way better than my first time in Denver.

For transportation, I made a down payment on

a 1952 Studebaker Land Cruiser, light green and set up a payment schedule. I also bought a TV on time. That's what you called making payments and using items before credit cards came into use. Small things you put on lay-a-way. The store would hold things until you finished all your payments, like buying a good suit or furniture. After you'd paid the full price, then you took the merchandise home. I think buying a car was one of the first times when people signed the contract, took possession of the item, then finished making payments—buying on time. If you didn't make your payments, they'd send someone to come collect whatever you'd gotten behind on.

In Colorado, I bluffed my way a lot on the job. I had a bit of knowledge, but could make it do— think things through and not rush into action.

I met a girl, the sister of a guy at work. We went to movies in Denver. She lived with her dad on a few acres at the edge of the city. She didn't have a mom at home, and wouldn't talk about her. The girl, Delores Petzold, worked as a housekeeper for people across the road from them. She had blondish hair and blue eyes. We fooled around some.

Delores and I got engaged. It was the thing to do in those days. You didn't just fool around with a good girl, you promised marriage. When we got engaged, I bought a set of rings on time.

We had some good times at my apartment, which had a separate entrance from the house. I used condoms for protection. She was a good person, nice, sociable—pleasant to be with. We talked a lot. One time I won some tickets to see the Harlem Globe Trotters. We both enjoyed that. But I felt inferior with Delores because she'd graduated from high school.

When I was nineteen, I got drafted.

In those days the Army and Air Force were united as the Army-Air Corps, the A-AC. I did eight weeks of Army-Air Corps basic training at Camp Chaffee, Arkansas. While there, Delores sent me a letter that she'd met someone else and broke off our engagement. If she didn't care for me enough to wait, that was fine with me. I asked for the rings back and she sent them to me. I sold them.

After basic training, the A-AC sent me to Lawton, Oklahoma to radio repair school. That was difficult, really difficult, but I made it through. Next, I got sent to St. Marcus, Texas to Gary Air Force School. There, I learned to be an aircraft and engine mechanic. I spent some time at Ft. Lewis, Washington, and then they sent me overseas, to Germany.

I wanted to be a pilot but only officers could be pilots. Even so, I learned some valuable skills while in the service and made a couple of lifelong friends.

While in Germany, something really big happened, an opportunity I couldn't pass up. I got my GED. It wasn't required by the A-AC; I just wanted to do it. The school was run by the A-AC but it was after hours and free for service men. I went to classes, studied, and passed the test.

There wasn't any graduation ceremony, but when they handed me the certificate, I felt good. Proud.

After one year and eleven months of service, I received an honorable discharge from the Army-Air Corps in March of 1955. I'd turned twenty-two the month before.

CHAPTER TWENTY

◆

While in the A-AC, I'd asked the money be sent to my mother that would have gone to my wife. That meant ninety dollars a month of my Class Q-D allotment went to my mother and I had thirty-three dollars a month for my personal use. That money helped my parents—my dad had moved home again—move beyond subsistence living on their Grade "C" dairy farm.

I still don't know why my mother let that mean man move back again and again. Maybe she felt it her duty as a wife and a Catholic. But I wouldn't have given him one penny, after his treatment of me, his only living son.

When the draft took me, I left behind debts—a car, the TV, and rings all bought on time. At that time there was the Soldiers and Sailors Relief Act and because of that Act, all payments on my debts stopped during my enlistment but had to be picked up again at the end of service. I'd traded the Studebaker for a 1949 six-cylinder, standard shift with overdrive, dark silvery grey Ford and owed $800 on it. I left the car with my mother. She didn't drive it much, just enough to keep the fluids going and the battery charged. Mostly, she kept it in a garage on the farm. She surprised me with some big news when I went to get the car. Somehow, she managed to negotiate what I owed down to $400. That was a huge help.

After buying the car and rings on time, I never went into debt like that again. From then on, I paid cash or used a credit card I could pay off each month. My rule of credit for me has paid off well. The burden of debts waiting for me after I finished my tour of duty became a worry.

Although I vowed to not go in debt again, I didn't give up on finding the right woman—a wife. When I was in my late twenties, I got engaged to a lady who was a member of the Assembly of God church. Because my family hadn't been regular church goers, she thought she was better than me. She'd make remarks now and then—jibes. Then she broke off the engagement and wanted to keep the rings.

I figured my hard-earned money entitled me to keep them. She wouldn't budge, so I talked to a lawyer, went to court and got the rings back. Later, I sold the rings for what I paid for them.

Don't lose money on any deal, my new motto.

After the A-AC tour, I had new confidence in my own skills. With my electrical background plus what I learned in the service, I found a job with Western Electric Company in Kansas City. They sent me around to install telephone switchboards.

Some of the lines were hot because the switchboards were in operation while I worked on them. That got interesting, but I did all right—watched to keep my hands in safe places.

From my base in Kansas City, I found a better paying job at Beverly Car & Finance Company. I became a repo man—repossessed cars from people who'd gotten behind on payments. It was a tough job in a lot of ways, but I learned some important things about finance, car titles, and repossession that helped me in later years, after I became self-employed.

After one year at as a repo man, I found a better position with Airmod Company.

Airmod was an airplane modification company. They'd refurbish planes for the Air Force and that's pretty much what I'd done in the A-AC. It was a job tailor made for me, in most ways. After not too long at Airmod, I got promoted to inspector.

Next, I went to work for Boeing Company and the Minuteman Missile program as an inspector. An inspector of missiles! Me, the scruffy kid whose parents gave him away. That thought still makes me smile. No one from my childhood days would have ever predicted I'd have a job with Boeing, and certainly never to be inspecting missiles. It was a really good job. Really good.

Boeing paid me well and it was actually easier work being an inspector than being one of the crew that worked on the missiles. The inspector just looked at others' work and filled out reports. Someone else had to fix any problems I found.

I had to go down into the silos and inspect

missiles around Northwest Missouri near Whiteman Air Force Base, and then traveled to Montana, and North Dakota. I worked for Boeing until I had saved fifty thousand dollars. That was 1968. Taking into account inflation, that fifty-thousand would be three hundred thousand dollars in 2014.

I was thirty-five.

CHAPTER TWENTY-ONE

After Boeing, I got into real estate working for a firm in Brookfield, Missouri. From my work as an electrician, I knew the country all around Northwest and Central Missouri. Right away, I decided to get my broker's license. A smart mouthed realtor, Lori King, told me I wasn't smart enough.

Oh yeah? I said to myself.

I went to Career School of Real Estate in Springfield, Missouri. In the same day, I passed the test for being a real estate agent, and I also passed the broker's test! That's an accomplishment I'm really proud of to this day. Lori King never congratulated me but I hadn't expected her to.

In my real estate work, I got acquainted with a man named Mike Tomlinson. He owned an insurance brokerage and also sold real estate in Breckenridge, a little town not far from Chillocothe, Missouri.

Small town and farm properties were in high demand. In the late nineteen-sixties, Kansas City had some bad race riots. It was a scary time in many ways, and a lot of people wanted to move out of the city to farms or small towns. Mike found properties and I bought them—farms, houses, small businesses. The largest farm he found was 160 acres. We'd put in bathrooms, septic tank systems, install kitchen sinks—fix up the houses and then sell them. Then I went out on my own, buying and selling properties.

My name got out and people started calling me to find a property.

Sometimes the farms had been vacant long enough that the yards and fields had grown wild. I bought a tractor and bush hog and cleaned up the outside, too. Sometimes I had six properties going at once, working on the houses, mowing the grass and generally modernizing the place. It kept me busy but I loved it. My nest egg from Boeing served me well.

I started to feel secure about my life.

Rehabbing properties was hard physical work, and hard mental work but I could see the payoff for my work right away. I had to keep good records of what I bought to fix up each place. And I had to do nice enough work so people would be attracted to the place, but most important, I had to make sure I could sell it for a profit. You didn't need to put gold plated fixtures in, just something new that worked. I'd buy at discount places and check things over to make sure all parts worked.

Sometimes I got into a fix I'd never imagined would happen. There was one property in central Missouri that had a patio out back. A maple tree had grown big and its roots cracked the patio. I was walking across the patio one time and almost stepped on a snake's tail as it went down the hole. I got a good look at the tail and backed off right quick. It was a rattlesnake! That thing had a den under the patio. Well, I wasn't about to sell a property with a rattlesnake living there so I had to get rid of that thing. Someone told me to put some diesel fuel down its den to drive it away. So I went to town and got some diesel and poured it down the snake hole. Sure enough, the snake disappeared.

Another time I bought a place that had thirty chickens so I had to keep them fed and protected. It was nice having the fresh eggs, but it became a big chore to keep track of those chickens. Each morning I'd let them out of the coop to forage. At night I'd put them in the coop or foxes would kill and eat the chickens and the eggs. Sometimes I'd not get there until after dark and there were no lights in the coop. You couldn't see if there was a snake—snakes loved eggs—or a possum or fox in the coop. I wouldn't go get the eggs after dark—not worth getting bit. I just shut the door and waited 'til morning to gather eggs and let the chickens out to forage.

Sometimes the house on a property would turn out to need more work than looked like from the outside. But if I spent a little more on one place, generally the next one would make up for it. Sometimes a place only needed a little cleaning up—new paint, new vinyl flooring in the kitchen and bathroom, that sort of thing. Consistently, I made money.

CHAPTER TWENTY-TWO

◆

After my two broken engagements, I wasn't too optimistic about marriage, but I dated lots of women. I always treated them with respect, and learned early on to give nice presents for birthdays and Christmas. My focus was on work. I'd long ago vowed to never be poor again. Money gives you leverage. Without money you're at the mercy of everyone.

My sister Margaret's marriage gave me encouragement. She went with friends to dances in Kansas City. One time she met a man named George Hawkins. She told me about him and one day she called while I was working at Rocky Mountain Arsenal.

"John, what do you think about George Hawkins?" Margaret asked.

"He's an all right fellow. You two have been dating a while now. Why do you ask?"

"He's proposed to me. Wants to get married. Do you think he'd be a good husband?"

"Yes, I do, Margaret. He's got a good income. Will be a good provider. And I think he's a good man. A kind man. Only problem is he smokes too much. But he's not a drinker so that's good."

I drove from Colorado to Kansas City for the wedding. They went to New Orleans on their honeymoon, her choice. I was happy for her.

Margaret and George lived in Kansas City. He was a builder. He and I always got along well. After I started working in real estate, he taught me a lot about the trades, especially plumbing. That helped me a lot with my property rehab work. For instance, he taught me how to use copper pipe to make good plumbing out of shoddy work, and to replace iron pipe plumbing you often found in those old places I was renovating.

I read newspapers all over the state, looking for foreclosures worth my investment.

On weekends, George would help me when there was something I couldn't figure out with one of my rehab places. I bought one house in Lebanon, Missouri that had sat vacant over winter with no heat and the pipes had all frozen. The owner was in jail for murder and the place was in foreclosure. The crime took place at a car lot in Springfield, not in the house, or I wouldn't have bought the place— would've made it hard to sell. After the shooting, the wife had gone to the state of Louisiana and abandoned the house.

The savings and loan that held the mortgage, after six months, foreclosed. According to the law, couldn't sell faster than that. The place had a second mortgage held by an individual. That individual didn't protect his mortgage during foreclosure proceedings, so he lost out when I bought from the S & L on the courthouse steps.

George helped me figure out what needed to be done to repair the plumbing on that house. It sold for a nice profit.

Early in my real estate work, I'd found you could make a good profit by buying a foreclosure. I read lots of different newspapers as I traveled around the state. After I fixed up the properties and sold them, I set a goal to make a twenty-five percent profit on each venture. Still do.

Today, I hold the first deed of trust on several properties all over Missouri—farms and houses in small towns, and some really big places. A first deed of trust is essentially the first mortgage; it takes precedence if the owner gets a second or third mortgage. That means I finance the sale up front.

My fifty thousand savings after I quit Boeing has multiplied many times over. One property alone, a nine hundred farm in prime farming country, brings me fifty thousand dollars in interest each year.

CHAPTER TWENTY-THREE

◆

Generally I get along with people, always have. It's my way of doing business—but I don't let anyone take advantage of me, either. You can smile a lot but still be a smart business person.

First time I had to take someone to court and foreclose on a property I'd financed was hard. I hated to do it, and had a lawyer write up the warning letter. I don't ever directly confront someone that's gotten behind. It's better for everyone to have it in writing from an authority. The letter gives them twenty-one days to get caught up with payments. If they can't do it, we foreclose. The lawyer selects a trustee to read off the notice of foreclosure at the court house door and take bids. I've bought many properties in that situation but haven't had to foreclose on too many of my own places. But if it is my property, I have to bid on it like anyone else.

In cases of bankruptcy, the whole thing has to go through bankruptcy court. Lots of paperwork. If the other person gets a lawyer, things can drag on and on. But the main thing is to keep a distance from the situation, not get personal. It's all business.

After the first time someone got behind on payments, I learned to write up my own paperwork, good as a lawyer's because it held up in court. One guy bought back his place, then got behind on payments and I foreclosed three times before he finally got it paid off.

A lot of people buying property from me couldn't have qualified for a bank loan so I've helped them get a home. Their own house. Their own farm. Their own business. I run my own credit report and decide whether they can make the payments.

CHAPTER TWENTY-FOUR

◆

It was during the late nineteen seventies, when I started making enough profit on real estate, that I set a goal of being a millionaire. Don't remember the exact date, but I was in my mid-forties and did the math, knew I could do it.

In 1993, my net worth hit one million. I didn't have a celebration, except my own satisfaction. That was big. Really big. That a kid with my upbringing—or lack of it could become a millionaire proves the American dream. Work hard, live frugally, pay attention to your business and you can make enough money in your good years to carry you in your senior years. I'm 83 now and still work every day.

I've never lost money on a property.

Sometimes I made less than my goal of twenty-five percent and sometimes I've doubled my money. I know how to spot the potential in a place. With most any house, if the foundation and roof are solid, that tells you the building is worth saving, even if the siding is rough, inside has ripped wall paper, there's no plumbing, no electricity and the linoleum is curled or ripped. Those things, including flooring, are just cosmetic. Fixable. Do your own labor and you've made enough money to sell the property and buy two more. They have TV shows these days that show people doing that all the time. Nowadays they call it flipping houses. I learned it by watching and doing years before those shows. But I've financed more than houses. I've also financed businesses and farms.

You need to know your business, and you need to know a lot about people. Although I met a few bad people—really bad people—as I made my way in the world, I met many more good people.

The first person in my memory who helped me other than relatives was Lloyd Townsend. He was the neighbor when we lived on the farm near Hamilton who saw my potential. I'd go visit the Townsends because they had several children, eight or so, and one was close to my age. Donald was a good friend. Mr. Townsend would talk to me, give me advice on how to get along in life. He talked to me like a person who could understand complicated things, and I appreciated that a lot. Because of his trust in me, the Townsend boys would invite me to go hunting with them. That was good, too—fun, interesting, and profitable.

The neighbor who helped me most understand business was Mr. Foley. He was the neighbor who gave me the sheep. He taught me how to care for the lambs, how to shear them, and where to take them to sell. He also taught me about bank accounts.

George Hawkins, my brother-in-law, taught me how to do plumbing and other building repairs—but mostly plumbing. That was a big help in my real estate days, when I finally made something of myself—made enough money to be independent. Then I made enough money to be called wealthy, at least by some standards. It would have been a lot harder without George.

In Denver, the man at the vegetable market who was nice saved my life in a way. He told me to go to ranch country where I'd have a chance at finding a job. He knew I wasn't ready for a big city like Denver.

When I worked at Rocky Mountain Arsenal, a man named Peterson helped me learn good carpentry. Peterson was older, maybe thirties or forties and I was just early twenties. For instance, he taught me how to drive big nails into corrugated roofing. That came in real handy when I started rehabbing properties years later.

In Oklahoma, where I'd gone to make some money during the wheat harvest, the couple who took me in as a hired hand were both really nice to me. I learned how much that means to someone newly out in the world—that not everyone is mean. Sometimes when you least expect it, you find some good people who are willing to help you.

There were some people in my life who really hindered me, although I eventually did well despite them.

My dad, Russell Garrison, was the worst example of a father I can imagine. He once took a loaded .22 rifle and threatened to kill me. We were arguing over something I can't even remember now. That man was just mean through and through. When he died, I paid for the funeral and his burial in Alta Vista cemetery, only because he was family.

The people who took me in as a foster child hurt me with their words and actions. They didn't hit me physically, but they treated me as worthless. I didn't take it – ran away. Somehow, I believed in myself, even if no one else did.

The man who abused me sexually hurt me, too—made me realize there were people in the world who were monsters. Couldn't imagine a grown man hurting a boy like that but I got away.

CHAPTER TWENTY-FIVE

◆

As a youngster, I learned when you saved your money you could get more with it than if you bought little things along the way. I've kept up the habit of saving as much as possible, not being extravagant with anything except maybe when I bought my first Cadillac. Even then, I'd learned about the wholesale price and the markup, and dickered the dealer down to what I thought was a fair deal. He might not have been happy, but he still made some money on the sale. I bought that Caddy in 1960 in Williamson, Kentucky and after I drove it a year or so, sold it for a profit in Kansas City.

In school, arithmetic came easy to me and that's helped in business. Grammar wasn't as much fun, but I did all right. And even though I didn't have any books at home as a kid, and not much in school, I've read a lot on my own. Sam Walton's autobiography is still one of my favorite books. I bought my own copy.

In the nineteen eighties, when the interest on

savings accounts started dropping, I started buying stocks. I didn't listen to someone trying to tell me about a great stock, I did my own research—bought old tried and true companies. My first stock purchase was Southern Company, an electrical holding company. Electricity was an easy stock choice, an obvious product whose demand grows as the population grows. I bought 500 shares of the stock at ten dollars a share. It doubled once.

Since then, I've bought Exxon, Conoco Phillips, Occidental Petroleum, Empire District Electric Company, and Walmart stocks. My 100 shares of Walmart stock have split so much I now hold 1600 shares.

Something else with stock, I've never sold any.

Even though my stocks have done well, I've made more money in real estate. These days, a very good personal and business friend, Roger Douglas, buys and owns the warranty deeds on most all my properties, but I hold the deeds of trust. Roger owned Douglas Realty in Lebanon, Missouri when I first met him. Over the years, we've bought many properties together. He is now my successor trustee for most properties.

As for cars, I've bought a new car every two years starting with when I worked for Boeing. I traveled a lot, so needed good transportation. But I've not lost money on cars; generally, I've made money on my sales by keeping the vehicles in prime condition. I've owned—in addition to three Caddys—Olds, Chevys, Fords, and a couple of Lincolns.

The biggest single boost toward accomplishing

my goal of being a millionaire came when Sam Davis, a banker in Cameron, Missouri, gave me a letter of credit. Most important, that letter of credit indicated no dollar amount of restrictions, and no time limit.

Reno and Jim Sonner of Air Mod Company believed in me, saw potential, and we became lifelong friends. Reno hailed from Lebanon, Missouri and moved there in his retirement. He became more like a father to me than anyone else in my life. His wife was a great friend, too.

Reno traveled all over the world with Air Mod. He was well educated and also wise. Some people are well educated, but don't apply their knowledge wisely; Reno did. He was thoughtful except he was a wild driver. His ability to think and his speed didn't go together. He'd drive 90 miles per hour on the highway. Fearless.

Reno lived a good life until well into his nineties. He was 96 when he passed. I still miss him.

CHAPTER TWENTY-SIX

◆

In 1975 I met the woman who helped me most with my professional and personal goals, other than my sister. I met Loraine Beeson at a real estate meeting in Springfield, Missouri and we immediately hit it off. There was a mysterious connection that happens only rarely between two people. We were married for twenty-five years and lived in Lebanon, Missouri. Lorene would jump into my rehab projects with as much enthusiasm as I had. She'd even get up on a roof to help make repairs.

One time we were painting the ceiling in a house and found our ladder was too short to reach the peaked part of the outside siding. We didn't have the time or inclination to go buy a longer ladder and it wasn't practical to get scaffolding— too expensive and too time consuming. So we devised an attachment to the handle of a paint brush and I backed my pickup close as I could get. I put the ladder on the pickup and managed to finish the job.

Loraine was a great cook with anything. I didn't have to eat bologna and crackers around her. She also loved to travel. One time we went to Las Vegas in our 1973 Chevelle, a tudor coupe. We got to Albuquerque and hit a blizzard. The road was blocked and we spent the night in the car. Soon as they got the highway clear, we went south and eventually made our way to Vegas. We went to shows but didn't gamble.

Lorene was older than me, but that didn't matter except she died too soon, in 2011. We were divorced then—my worst mistake—but remained best friends until she passed.

George Hawkins died of lung cancer 1978. All that smoking. Margaret lived to be eighty-nine. She had developed Alzheimer's and lived in a nursing home for a few years. Then she developed cancer and she died in December, 2012.

My nephews live in the Kansas City area. One is a CPA who worked for the IRS and the other is in insurance. I still see them every once in a while, just to keep in touch with family.

My dad died of colon cancer. He and Mom were living in an old house in Cameron, Missouri and were on SSI.

Mom lived with me for a time, and then moved into a nursing home in Lebanon, Missouri. One day she had a stroke. She'd just finished lunch. She coughed a little and fell over, dead. I paid for her funeral and her burial in Alta Vista cemetery. Put her next to Dad. That was in 1979.

CHAPTER TWENTY-SEVEN

◆

While I was living in Kansas City, I got my private pilot's license. Couldn't be a pilot in the Air Force, so I did it as a civilian. Don't know why, but I always wanted to fly. At the time I got my license, I worked for a man who owned his own plane. We flew all over the U.S. to do business. He had a large mobile home company. I love flying.

There is one person besides my mother who I've helped quite a lot over the years. We eventually bought a plane together. Laverne Alderton worked for me when I bought a gas station and used car lot in Buckner, Missouri. We got along real well and over the years I helped him out in different ways. He appreciated the help, and repaid me in kind. We owned a Piper Tripacer plane together. We kept it in a hangar in Brookfield.

One time I rented an Aronicka plane. That plane had a Model A car engine, a nightmare to keep going. I had to set that thing down in a cow pasture once. Laverne was with me. Turned out the fuel gauge didn't work. It showed I had half a tank of gas but I didn't have that much. Ran out of gas in the air and had to set down real quick. Fortunately, I located a field big enough for landing the plane. We hitch hiked to a place where we could get fuel, got a lift back to the plane, refueled, then flew that thing back to the airport.

Margaret and George had two boys. The boys liked to go flying with me. It was one of few luxury items for me, flying. But now that I've had heart problems, I can't pass the yearly physical to keep my license current. I miss flying.

CHAPTER TWENTY-EIGHT

◆

Flooring cars is an interesting and profitable small business venture. Sometimes a guy will buy a car at auction, fix it up, rent floor space at a dealership and sell the car. I loan him the money to buy the car at the auction—that's flooring the car. The guy then has to sell it. I charge him something for interest each month and when he sells the car, he pays me off in full.

One time a man switched titles and tried to cut me out of my money. I could have had him jailed, because the amount of money involved was felony level. But if I'd done that, I'd have been out my forty-four thousand. So we worked out a payment schedule. I got my money, and he stayed out of jail.

Over the years, I've floored many cars. I worked with one person mostly, Laverne Wagner in Lebanon, Missouri.

CHAPTER TWENTY-NINE

◆

When you get to a certain age, you think back about life. You think about your contributions to the world. The most important legacy for me is that I've financed home purchases for people who couldn't get credit at a bank.

Some of my mortgagees have filed bankruptcy so a bank or savings and loan wouldn't talk to them about financing a home. But I always do my own credit check and look at their credit worthiness in a different way. I loan only fifty percent of the selling price of the property, so if the person can't make payments, the property is still worth enough that I don't lose money.

In my way of thinking, that's a pretty strong legacy, something good I've done for my place in this world—to help people own a home. That's the traditional American dream and I think it's a good one. Everyone needs to have a dream come true. Everyone needs help making their dream come true. I've helped several people fulfill their dream.

CHAPTER THIRTY

◆

In business dealings, many people have asked me to invest in their enterprises. Everyone seems to have a favorite cause. I decided to donate some money to College of the Ozarks. All students at the College work for their tuition, room, and board. I admire that—working and earning your way through school. To thank me for my donation, the College put my name on the front of the new Activities Center, which they built as an attachment to the Keeter Center athletics complex.

John A. Garrison, age 23. He was working for
AirMod Company at the time of this photograph

John Garrison is center front. This is the only
photograph he has of himself as a child.

ABOUT THE AUTHOR

Joyce C. Ragland is the author of more than one hundred publications including academic books, professional articles, short stories, poetry and nonfiction books.

Throwaway Child, the Life Story of John A. Garrison tells the story of a child whose parents gave him away at age eleven, but his resilience gave him strength to set high goals and achieve great success in life.

After a career as teacher, professor, and assistant dean, Ragland now finds time for her lifelong love of creative writing. Joyce is founder and president of the Ella Ragland Art charity and raises funds for local Alzheimer patient projects.

She resides in Springfield, Missouri with a canine companion, Bessie Jo, a short-haired Border Collie.

AUTHOR NOTES

To learn about John Garrison's life, I first let him talk, to say what he first needed to get off his mind. We met several times to follow up, and I asked him many questions. Some of the questions and answers follow.

In your youth, what gave you hope?

"I kept looking for more opportunity, better wages. I often did that by doing a job that someone else couldn't or wouldn't do, like operating the combine for the man who'd been crippled by polio."

When did you have your first candy?

"I was ten years old and my sister was nineteen and had a job. She bought me some penny candy folded in squares with four in a packet. She also bought me my first ice cream on a stick and my first bottle of pop. I still remember how it burned when you let the pop get under your tongue."

If you had run into yourself at age 15-16 would you have liked the guy?

"I think I would. I'd liked his knowledge and ability to get things accomplished. I don't believe in whining. Have no time for complainers."

What is your best memory?

"My first solo flight."

What was your most embarrassing thing?
"One time my billfold wasn't in my pocket and I thought a friend of mom's that was a drinker took it. Later, I found the billfold."

What was your greatest fear?
"One time I saw a mountain lion on a ridge above a stream. Those things are unpredictable."

What is your most treasured possession, and why?
"Money. It gets you through doors."

If you could change one thing about yourself, what would that be?
"Education. I'd have gotten at least four years of college."

What are three words to describe you?
"Frugal. Determined. Adventurous."

What's the most evil thing any person can do?
"Take advantage of a child."

Do you have any prejudices?
"I guess everybody does."

What are your favorite movies?

"Westerns, and adventure series like Alaska travel."

What have you done that you are not proud of?

"Before I was of legal age, I bought a car, drove it but did not make payments and when they came to get it I disaffirmed the contract, went to court and got my down payment back. The owner got his car back, but it was used."

Are you spontaneous, or do you need to have a plan?

"A plan. I like to think things out first."

What do you want the reader of this book to get from it?

"Encouragement. To know that you *can* be successful."

On January 19, 2014, CBS News reported that only five percent of American households are millionaire status.

Another Publication by Joyce C. Ragland

DRED THE FRED

Dread the FRED tells the story of a team of students in the small Conway Missouri high school who overcame huge obstacles to dominate a national robotics competition.